Poems of Elly Gross
Memories of a Holocaust Survivor

Author and Publisher
Elly Berkovits Gross

Printed In Canada

Poems of Elly Gross,
Memories of a Holocaust Survivor
by Elly Berkovits Gross
First Edition published by Melvin I Weiss Esq.
*Printed by Columbia House Inc.
ISBN 909713639-0-0

Other books by Elly Gross, Author/Publisher

Storm Against the Innocents,
Holocaust Memories and Other Stories
ISBN 0-9713639-1-9 Copyright @ 2003
Elly Gross, nee Berkovits
Library of Congress Number 2003097136
* Printed in Canada

Infernos thes Innocentes In Spanish
ISBN 0971363935 Published by Farkas family
Library of Congress Number 2004097099
translated Liuba Libensky & Marcela Oliden
Copyright in Spanish by author to Farkas family
* Printed in Santiago, Chile

Elka's Growing Up In A Changing World
ISBN 0971363927 Copyright @ 2004
Elly Berkovits Gross
Library of Congress Number 2004090485
* Printed in Canada

Revised Second Edition
Poems of Elly Gross,
Memories of a Holocaust Survivor
ISBN 0971363943 Copyright @ 2005
Library of Congress Control Number 2005904954
*Printed in Canada

Table of Contents

Some of these poems are about the life of my family prior to the Second World War, others reflections on personal experiences from the Holocaust and thereafter. In 1998, 1999, 2000 & 2004. I was in Auschwitz-2/Birkenau, Majdanek, Sandomirz, Tykochin & Varsauw.

Prologue   I   by Melvin I Weiss, Esq.
Letters   II. III. IV.V.   by Gabriel and Jonathan
Documents VI.   received after liberation

02. My Mother's Flowers.......... In memory of my mother
04. I Went to Kindergarten................ Childhood Memory
06. My Hometown.................. Childhood Remembrances
08. My Only Doll........................ A Child happiness & loss
10. My First Dancing Class.................. A Child's Sad Day
12. Cold and Icy Day......................... Frozen Winter Day
14. My Only Brother............................... Broken Dreams
16. The Storm that Struck Europe....... European History
18. Hungarian Invasion............ Tragedies of Hung. rules
20. Russian Hills........................ In Memory of My Father
22. Miss Did A Star Fall On Yo
                          ....Jews Lose Citizens Rights
24. Where I Can Find Some Mazel
                              .... Searching for Luck
25. We Made Matzo.................. In Memory of My Granny
26. Where is G'd?... Arrival in Hell
28. The Echo and Chaos............. Separation from family
30. There is no Bird or Butterfly
                              .... Memory of Birkenau
32. Why I Did Not Say, "Mommy Please Come With Me"
                              .... Holocaust Quilt Memories

34. Shower In Birkenau......... My 1'st Shower in Birkenau
36. Roll Call In Birkenau.................. Memories of roll call
38. In Birkenau Miri Saved.......How I Survived Birkenau
40. Jews from Czechoslovakia...I have seen
     .... Terezin Jews
42. The Rooster is Calling Good Morning
     ....Jews Awaiting Messiah
44. Homecoming..................... A Survivor Returns Home
46. Our Daughter..................................Our Daughter
48. Chibi the Little Chick......................... Our Son
50. Left Our Homeland to the Unknown
     .... Everything Lost New Begin
52. Going to College................. I tried to improve myself
54. The Golden Age........................... Elders Hardship
55. When Stricken by Stroke.....My husband had a CVA
58. In Memory of Our Martyrs!....Remembering Martyrs
60. My Vision in Sandomirz......... I've been at that Plaza
62. Birds in Majdanek................... Statue in Majdanek
64. Mother with Her Child........ Symbol of Mother's Love
66. Listen to the Winds........... Mass Grave in the Forest
68. Treblinka.....................................J. Korcza's orphans
70. (Not) Every Life Returns in Birkenau.
     ....Life in Birkenau's C.Camp
72. My Heart Aches............................ My life time pain
74. The Grass is Green.................. Blood soaked grass
76. The Long Row of Blue Jackets
     ....Jewish youth in blue jkts
78. The Little Lonely Child!............ A child left alone
80. Letter to My Mother!.............. I remember my mother
82. Whose Hair is on Display?
     ....Victims Hair in Auschwitz
84. Luggage, Silent Witness ...Victims name on luggage
86. Symphony Music in Birkenau....Slaves played music
88. A Former Paratrooper........Former Nazi soldier in NY
89. Celebration in Cesarea... Jews in the Roman theater
91. My Husband Story...... forced labor & Death March
93. Epilogue..

PROLOGUE

Elly came into my office in the winter of 1998 bearing a smile on her sweet face; a smile I later realized is permanently affixed to cloak the unimaginable remembrances of a past so horrible that they transcend our ability to comprehend.

This Holocaust survivor, at the age of 15 was transported from her home in Şimleu-Silvaniei, Transylvania, with her 37 year old mother and 5 year old brother to Auschwitz - by cattle car. On their arrival they were unloaded, with hundreds of others, only to be separated - one group to the left the other to the right - by a Nazi officer wearing white gloves. Elly later learned that officer was Dr. Josef Mengele, the infamous Nazi Doctor who used human beings as medical guinea pigs. Elly wound up on the right, her mother and brother on the left. Elly never again saw them alive.

After surviving over a year in several concentration camps, including Auschwitz, and working as a slave laborer at a Volkswagen plant, Elly was freed by the Allies and went back to Romania, married, had a son and daughter, and later moved to the United States. Fifty years later, she participated, with teenagers from the United States, in the March of the Living, visiting Auschwitz and waking with the youths to the site of the murders, where she saw photographs of vicious images that she has endured every day of her life, those of the concentration camp and her life as a slave laborer.

But, a particular photograph stood out among the others. First she spotted the white gloves that by a wave to the left, separated her forever from her loved ones. Then, Elly was thunderstruck by the picture of her mother, holding her young brother in her arms, standing in front of the railroad cars, surrounded by hundreds of other prisoners. Rendered speechless, numbed by the vision that she thought would carry forever only in her memory, Elly went home and started to write. She spoke little, but wrote much. She wrote poems which I published for her.

Melvyn I. Weiss

NOW, the reprint Elly published herself, because of how deeply she cares about creating a lasting monument to those who suffered and survived - of didn't survive.

To merely call Elly Gross an impressive woman is such an understatement as to be ludicrous. Though she lost her entire family to the great evil of the century, while she endured the life of a slave laborer in a filthy factory, she survived. She returned home to nothing in Romania, but married a man named Ernest and began a life and family. They eventually left Romania, along with the Communist regime there, and moved to New York City. Not really even being able to speak the language, Elly and Ernest Gross again began with nothing.

While they were able to provide educations for their children, they were too busy to do so for themselves. But much later, after retirement, Elly got her GED and went on to get an Associate's degree with major in Fine Arts from LaGuardia College. But just educating herself was not enough. She began speaking at schools about her experiences, to ensure that the horror of just over fifty years ago would not be forgotten. She was a plaintiff in a lawsuit against the company who callously used her and so many others to be slave laborers, promising any compensation to charity before the lawsuit even began.

She went on trips such as The March of the Living, in which she helped to ensure that young people truly understood just what her experiences were in the places where they happened. And she has written countless poems, of which this text is just a small sample. She has never gotten over the loss of her parents and especially her brother, but the joy that she has found in the family that she created is evident in the pieces about her son and daughter. It is evident in the way that she both educates about the past working towards the future.

As her grandson, I (along with, of course, my brother) was welcome overnight guest at my grandparents' house every weekend, during which in the evening and morning she always asked, "What can I make for you?" though she often said "When I was 16..." late night. I remember when my grandmother retired, and then when she challenged herself with college (right when I did), and I remember her triumph when she succeeded. I was born well after her great trial, but through her stories I know much of what she has experienced, and I will remember. So will everyone who reads this book.
Gabriel Weisz

Elly Gross, nee Berkovits has always led a life of many roles, rapidly metamorphosing from student to prisoner of war, then from freed slave to bride housewife to business woman, from mother to caretaker. Throughout all these roles, one characteristic remained constant. Elly Gross is a Survivor. She is a survivor of the war which shattered all of the nations and conventions of Europe and the atrocious death camps where undesirable were swept away, of the ensuing struggle after the war to regain a foothold in normal society. A survivor of the turmoil of the communist regime in Romania and of the flight from there to a hopeful land of opportunity. Elly's unique unbrea-kable spirit upheld her through triumph and tragedy, and enabled her to bring her children to realize the fullest potential of the American dream.

Now, she spends her time taking care of her husband, who unfortunately suffered a stroke several years ago, bullying her various descendants like any good Jewish grandmother must, and reflecting on her past. This book is a compilation of her reflections on those events sprinkled with her perspective of the tragedies of modern years. In her immigrant's simple, yet powerful language she lets us share the voyage through the most troubled years of the century and allows us to feel, on a very fundamental level, the powerful nobility of that unusual creature: my granny, the Survivor.
Jonathan Weisz

Documents I received in 1945 after liberation

Dedicated to
my parents and brother
and all other
victims of the Holocaust.

Content of this book are about the author's experiences prior, during and after the Holocaust.

The second edition was revised by Chen Liang, William O'Malley, Melissa Chardon. Photo scans by Jonathan Weisz, Melissa Chardon and Lavaughn Brathwaite.
Final arrangement by David Soltanovici.
Without them this book would not be reprinted.

A special thanks from the author.

Elly Berkovits Gross

Elly Berkovits Gross

My Mother's Flowers

My mother loves flowers
and plants them every spring.
Her morning glory
climbs on a string.

With green leaves
and colorful flowers,
the morning glory makes
shadows on our open hallway.

My mother loves
the Japanese lily;
it blooms with white flowers,
with strong fragrance.

My mother loves the dahlia;
some name it "the pauper flower,"
with its bright colored flowers
open late summer into autumn.

Mother loves zinnias too,
in rainbow colors,
all-summer sprouting
cutting flowers.

My mother also likes portulaca.
It grows in sand or stone,
and blooms as a colorful blanket
covering the ground.

Another of my mother's favorites
is the rooster head.
The flowers are dark red
and bloom all summer.

My mother loves
every flower in any color.
In her small garden,
flowers always bloom.

Mother takes care of
her beautiful flowers,
and the air is filled
with fragrance.

The Author's Mother,
Irina Berkovits
(1906-1944)

I Went to Kindergarten

With a blue bow in my hair
and a lunch bag in my hand.
I went to the kindergarten
on a windy, cloudy day.

As I got close to the nursery
a little rain sprinkled.
But I was not too wet as
I walked in the long hallway.

Another girl entered with
an umbrella in her hand.
My umbrella was home.
As desperate as I was,-

Standing on my toes, I opened
the door, and in the pouring
rain ran out crying, to return
home through the pouring rain.

My parents' neighbor's son
saw me on the rainy street.
He asked "Why are you crying?"
"What is wrong?"

Sobbing hysterically, I
explained that one girl
came with an umbrella
to kindergarten.

And I did not have one,
so I had to return home
to bring my umbrella.
He took me home in his arms.

I will never forget this
episode as long as I live.
How foolishly a child's mind works!

Already arrived at the nursery;
Crying, I run out in the rain,
and got soaking wet for an umbrel-
la. Soon the rain stopped and
the sun shone in the blue sky.

What a silly child I was.
Mother changed my wet clothes.
Smiling, she put me into bed, and

I cried bitterly as I fell asleep.
The Author at two years old

My Hometown

Șimleu-Silvaniei, where I was born, I remember as a beautiful City. The city lies in a valley, surrounded by the "Meses Mountain." All year round, there is snow on the mountain.

I remember, in the summer when it rained, or when the sun shone very bright, some snow melted. The city's river, the Crasna rapidly rose, overflowing its banks.

Muddy water covered the left side of my hometown. People packed away, and moved to higher ground. The muddy water swept away everything in its path.

I lived on the right side of the river by the "Măgura Hills." From the "High Hills of the Măgura" a small stream with crystal clear water flowed slowly down the middle of my street.

In the middle of the paved street, in the summer's warm weather my friends and I dammed the water with sand, to create our own lake. We floated our paper boats on the lake.

Proud "sailors" made from matches navigated the boats on our lake. Those paper boats soaked and soon sank. The one whose boat went under first was the loser in that game.

Our fun turned sour when it rained or when the snow melted. The stream grew angry and big. Water covered our street from one side to the other; carried stones and broken trees.

When it got cold the water froze, and created side to side a frozen street. We children hurried to go on ice.

Our mothers worried that we kids would get frostbite.
It never bothered us.

My Only Dolly

Twice a year, with Mother, we visited my grandmother. Granny lived in another town, so she seldom had a chance to see us. Her other seven grandchildren visited her almost every day. And as some grandmothers do, she criticized them for everything.

Grandmother loved me a lot,
but she never gave me a gift.
In the 1930's, very few could
spend money on presents.
Families could not buy gifts,
or toys. They were satisfied
to make ends meet.

We children created our toys
from wild chestnuts, matches,
beans, ropes, strings,
wild flowers, and stones.

Once, when my friend's father traveled, he brought my friend furniture for dolls. Although my father always worked, he had no money for presents or toys.

One time my father traveled
too, and he brought me
a beautiful doll.
I was happy and felt "in heaven."
She had a porcelain face,
blonde hair.

I ran to my friend with my new gift, and suggested that we should play with her furniture and my doll. She said, "Let me see your doll." I put my beautiful doll in her hand. Then she hit it on the side of a wood barrel and broke my only doll's nose. Devastated as I was, I ran home crying.

Mother said, "If you do not like that she broke your doll's nose, do not play with her anymore."

Mother was smart!

Next day, we played together, again. We tried to repair the doll's nose. My friend was a doctor, and I was a nurse. We could not repair the broken nose.

I never got another doll. There was no money for toys!

As I aged, I realized, I never had a truly good friend.

My First Dancing Class

In my hometown, my aunt's younger brother opened a dancing school for teenagers. With a few of my friends we registered for classes.

We learned how to dance gracefully and not step on our partners' toes. Some of my friends had prior dance instruction.

For them it was easy to follow the music rhythm and dance gracefully.

At my first dance lesson, I was a clumsy young child. Not many boys asked me for a dance.

My disappointment increased as heavy storm clouds darkened the sky. It thundered and lightning hit the dance hall. Electric wiring burned, and we were in complete darkness.

Heavy rain with egg size hail covered the ground. I was scared and miserable.

I started to cry hysterically, "Please, someone help me get home to my mother."

Who wants to walk in a heavy storm with a crying girl?

During the storm, hail over twenty centimeters thick—close to a foot—covered the ground.

The heavy storm knocked out trees, electric and telephone lines. On streets, it was hazardous and difficult to walk.

Ice covered the streets.

People shoveled hail for hours and made piles of ice. As the storm raged no one danced and everyone's time ruined.

Cold and Icy Day

In my hometown,
winter begins in about
October every year.
First, it's cold, rainy,
and windy; then,
rain freezes on the street.

It's treacherous
to walk on icy roads.
It does not matter,
in rain or cold, the freezing
weather does not stop children
from going to school.

Parents worry that their
children might fall
on the slippery paths.
In dangerous weather,
parents walk their
children to school.

My father worried that
I might fall,
so he got ready
to come with me
going to school,
on a cold, rainy,
frozen day.

Frozen rain created
ice on streets.
To protect me,
my father held a cane
in one hand
and with his other,
held my hand.

He balanced himself
with his cane.

The street was shiny
with frozen rain.
Father slipped
on the slippery
ice and fell backwards
on the ground.

He hit his back
and head hard. I tried
to help him to get up,
but he was big
and I was small.

Crying, I asked people
for help, but not many
walked on the street.

From the bakery across
the street someone
came to help my father up
from the icy frozen street.

Luckily my daddy
got only bruises.
With no escort
I got to school.
Our teachers
dismissed classes early.

The sun smiled
and melted the ice.
Soon there was none
left on the street.

My Only Brother

I was a lonely single child
and jealous of my friends.
Of those who had a brother
or a sister with whom to play.
I felt small and very alone.

When I was ten years old my
little brother was born.
He was handsome, with black hair,
red cheeks and black eyes.
I was happy to have a brother.

I loved the little boy
and he liked to be with me.
He took his first steps,
balanced with his hands and
with a smile, he ran into my arms.

I felt so joyous that I cried.
The boy was close to my heart.
It gave me great satisfaction
when our mother trusted
my little brother to my care.

I planned to go together with
him to the park when he grew up
and on the hills to pick wild
strawberries, blackberries and
wild flowers for our mother.

Our father also had plans for
his only son's bar-mitzvah,
the school the boy would attend.
Maybe he would be a doctor,
perhaps a lawyer or a mechanic.

In the spring, when my brother was born, the Nazis invaded Czechoslovakia.

The winds of the Second World War began to blow over our heads, but no one could have imagined what followed next.

Fate changed our family's life, and our dreams did not come true. In the stormy winds of Europe, our hopes were demolished, and again...

I remained a single lonely child.

The Author's Brother,
Adalbert Berkovits 1939-1944

The Storm that Struck Europe

Those who were born in the late 1920's or in the 1930's missed the prior, worry-free life. But the problem started much before, when the breeze of World War I began - it was in the early 1910's.

Many people died during the war, and life afterwards was difficult. Depression rose high, whose fault was it? Easy to blame a group of people. Where to find a nation that can be blamed for a difficult and harsh life?

It must be a nation without a homeland, a group of people who have no country, who cannot say, "We have a country, a homeland." This nation is free prey, and the Depression can be blamed on them. They have no country on earth to go to.

By blaming Jews in the 1920 and 1930's a lunatic of the era united his people.

The slogan, "Kill the Jews" was music to the Nazis and collaborators ears. In the storm that swept through Europe, Jews were such easy prey. No homeland, no country where Jews could go. In this storm my people were robbed of their possessions and their lives.

For the few of us who survived with broken hearts, our homeland, Israel, is the cure for our destroyed lives. Small and strong, Israel, is a beautiful country where we Jews can go to mend our broken hearts.

Now we can say with heads held high and pride in our hearts, "We have a country. We have a homeland. We will not allow it to happen again that Jews around the world be easy prey."

We have the State of Israel, a place to go.

Hungarian Invasion

People in Europe were suffering:
everyone was struggling.
Depression is like the locust,
that eats up everything in its
path, as after fire, only bare
ground remains.

In the market there was plenty
of food, but very few had money
to buy. No work! No income!
Even though life was harsh,
we were home together,
and we had our freedom.

Soon more problems arose.
On September 10, 1940,
the Hungarian invasion brought
devastation to local people.
The new government seized
treasures, looted everything.

Took over the border to the mainland. Life day by day got harder.
From their homeland Hungarian's
brought misery. Coupons were
distributed. Food, clothing, and
shoes were given by ration only.
And for the lack of goods,
Jews were blamed.

The government seized Jewish
belongings and property, and gave
them free to loyal Hungarian's.
Local Hungarian's were happy for
a while, but they got greedy
and demanded more.

Harsh new laws hit the Jews.
Restrictions were issued for
travel and schooling; curfews
were implemented, men drafted
into forced labor, and other
injustices. Still the Hungarian's
were not content; they wanted
more.

It was spring. It was warm.
The sun was shining.
Meadows were green.
Trees and flowers
were blooming, but for the Jews
it was dark and cloudy.

To appease the locals
and the Germans, the Hungarian
government forced Jews out of their
homes, out of their cities.
And in a hurry, gave Jews to the
Nazi Germans.

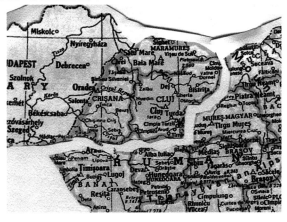

Three regions, Bihor/Crişan, Cluj,
Maramureş were attached to Hungary
September 10, 1940

Russian Hills

Beside Russian Hills,
a forced labor worker is marching.
Be careful, dear worker,
do not step on a mine.

Russians place mines
to protect their homeland.
The Huns/German Nazis
are invaders on Russian lands.

The Nazis drafted Jews
into forced labor camps.
They make them walk through minefields,
and not care how many died.

In one of these forced labor unit
is my dear father, too.
I pray every day to G'd
that my father's life be saved.

Please, G'd, watch his unit,
watch over on my father,
so that he doesn't step on mines,
beside Russian Hills.

To keep him warm I knit
sweaters and socks.
My mother prepares packages
to sends to my father's unit.

We anxiously await a letter,
which never arrives.
How would we know that my father
received the warm clothes?

Please, G'd, take care of all
those in forced labor units, and
help them return to their homes,
from beside the Russian Hills.

Oh, G'd, hear, listen to my
prayers and save my father's life.
Please look after my father
so that he won't step on a mine.

Over two years passed when I was
told that my father was burned
alive. With his fellow laborers
he perished, beside the Russian
Hills.

The Author's Father
Eugene Berkovits
(1905-1943)

Miss, Did A Star Fall On You?

After the Hungarian invasion
of September 10, 1940,
we Jews were deprived
of citizens' rights.

In 1944 the Hungarian
Government issued a decree
that we Jews must wear
a yellow Star of David.

With the yellow patch
on our left chest
we Jews were labeled
with the Star of David.

The local population
could recognize a fearful
Jew from far away
on the city's street.

Locals called to us "dirty Jew –
a star fall on you?"
They freely spit on Jews,
and some Jews were beaten.

That I was born a Jew
was a daily shame.
Yesterday's friends asked:
"Miss, did a Star fall on you?"

Even though I was the same
Jewish child on our street
with whom they had grown up
and played for many years.

A question still remains:
Did Jewish leaders know about
the laws that were being made
against the Jews?

Jews daily had fewer,
and fewer citizens' rights.
No one ever will know
how much our leaders knew.

Jewish women, selected to labor.
Auschwitz-2/Birkenau, June 2, 1944

Where Can I Find Some Mazel?

"Mazel' means luck in English,
why does not everyone have mazel?
When you have your health
and food to eat, it's mazel.

But we human beings wish to have
more than just food to eat.
We need some happiness
in life for healthy mazel.

When one gets married,
the new couple has mazel.
When a healthy child is born
the new parents have mazel.

I wish to buy some mazel,
but nowhere is it for sale.
In store or in a market,
no one can buy mazel.

When someone trips while walking,
but doesn't fall; it's mazel.
Someone wins the lotto jackpot
and gets rich has had mazel.

But someone who get sick
and for weeks lies in bed
doesn't have too much mazel.
When he recovers, it's mazel.

Very few are born with mazel
and others all their life
struggle for a little mazel.
Nowhere is mazel for sale.

When children have success
their parents have mazel.
No matter how much one wants
to pay, one can't buy mazel.

We Made Matzo

The Hungarian authorities forbade Jews to make or import matzo. Granny and her son outsmarted the law. They called Granny's brother and they figured how to make and bake matzo.

They washed the grain, then dried it in the sun, and afterwards ground it. There was plenty of flour for matzo. Grandmother got new wood and smoothed the wood with glass. Then grandmother gathered the family to make the matzo.

Her brother made the dough and we grandchildren rolled the dough on the new wood table. When we rolled the matzo dough the pieces that got wrinkled were not kosher for Passover. The boys gave the wrinkled dough to the chickens in the backyard.

After rolling each ball of dough we had to scrape the table with a piece of clean glass. When we rolled the matzo, we got blisters on our hand. Grandmother and her brother heated a large brick oven using chopped wood, and the family helped to make and bake the matzo.

Granny outsmarted the law Hungarian's imposed on Jews. She her son and her brother helped the family to have kosher matzo. This was my family's last Passover.

Where Is G-d?

The sun shines bright,
but it is dark.
Smoke covers the sky,
so I can't see the sky.
Why is it so dark?

Ashes and fire arise
from the ground,
but there is
no fire around.

Oh yes, there are
five chimneys which
pour smoke with ashes
and darken the sky.

Goes up, up high in the air.
What could be there?
Heavy smell everywhere.
Is a rubber factory there?

Oh no, no,
my soul, my heart
goes to heaven.
Oh G-d, are you there?

Please open
the gate to paradise;
let my soul, my heart
enter heaven.

My heart breaks
and I ask why?
Where is our G-d?

June 2, 1944, as deportees. We
arrived in Auschwitz-2/Birkenau
"Arbit Macht Frei"
"Works makes you free"
The date gate at railroad tracks

Echo and Chaos

I hear the echo of children's
cries: "Mommy, I am hungry." "Do
not cry, my child," Mother said.
She holds and kisses her child,
but she does not have any food,
or water, to give to her child.

Dogs on leashes bark,
men in striped uniforms
whisper, and soldiers scream:
"Fast, fast, stinky Jew."
Such a chaos on the ramp.
What is happening?

Locked for six days
without food and water.
My mother holds in her
arms my weakened brother.
A man in uniform with white
gloves waves right and left.

Points my mother and brother
to the left and me and others
to the right.
In the chaos, I ask,
"When will I see my mother again?"
A Kapo said,
"Sunday at the family reunion."

Over a year passed,
and that Sunday never came.

That blasted day of June 2, 1944,
I waved goodbye to my mother
and brother. The echo and chaos
I hear and see every day as if
it happened today.

On April 23, 1998, not Sunday,
but Thursday, in Birkenau
Lager D on a large display,
a mother holds a child in her arms.
And I see my mother, my brother.
So I do have a family reunion.

How can I reverse time to see them
alive, and try to go with them to
the left? The echo and chaos
forever ring in my ears.
Can anyone understand my pain?

Auschwitz-2/Birkenau disembarkment ramp
The Small boy with the beret and the
woman holding him are the Author's mother
and brother June 2, 1944

There is No Bird Or Butterfly

Barbed wire with high voltage,
and watch towers with soldiers.
I can see only four tall chimneys,
which pour ash and fire.

The air is full of heavy smoke;
it smells like burned rubber.
I can never see the sun,
because the sky is blurry.

When the sun shines,
it is still cloudy
and when it rains,
the ground is muddy.
I walk on sand and stone.
There is no grass or tree.

If some green would grow,
without any shame,
I would pick it to eat—
even at the risk of being killed.

I am enclosed with
my fellow inmates.
Our crime is that
we were born Jews.
This place is forgotten
by everyone in the world.

The Nazis and collaborators
robbed us of everything:
our freedom, our possessions,
and ultimately,
our families' lives.

Our relatives are gassed, burned,
their ashes thrown in the river.

We who were selected to the right
are only temporary survivors.

Birds and butterflies never fly;
they do not like smoke in the air.
I always wished to be a bird,
so I could fly away.

To leave this sad place,
and go home to my parents.
But I did not have wings
to fly like a bird or butterfly.

"Why I Did Not Say, Mommy Please Come With Me?"

On May 27, 1944, my mother, brother and I were strip-searched, then forced into a boxcar with about ninety to one hundred strangers, without food, water, or even air. The convoy of many boxcars started to roll.

On Friday, June 2, 1944, the transport suddenly halted and the doors were opened. Men in striped rags jumped into our boxcar. One whispered to me, "Say you are eighteen," and to my mother, "Give the boy to someone." I thought, "Are these men lunatics?"

The men pushed old people and children. Sick and dead were thrown on the same truck. I thought, "What is wrong? Are they mad?" Mother asked, "What should we do?" I said, "We cannot give my brother to strangers. He is five years old, and I am fifteen."

It happened as fast as lighting; there was no time to think. I was pushed to the right. My mother, holding my brother in her arms, remained in the left lane. As I ran to reach the others I waved to them. They looked in the direction in which I had departed.

I relive this moment all my life. During my life as problems arise, it crosses my mind that I did wrong, and tormented with remorse. Why didn't I say to my mother, "Give my brother to anyone and come with me." Why do I feel guilt that mother was sent to the left?

In my life, tragedies poured on me. I was robbed of my father at age thirteen. When I was fourteen, he perished in a forced labor camp. When I was fifteen, my mother and brother were taken away from me.
Was I selfish or not?
Was what I did wrong?

If I could change the time I would not care that my brother was only five years old. I would say, "Mommy, give my brother to any- one." Why did I not say, "Mommy, please come with me."

You reader, be the judge. Why can I not forget? What punishment do I deserve? Was it my crime?

Disembarkment ramp Auschwitz-2/Birkenau
June 2, 1944*

Shower in Birkenau

A new train of deportees arrived
and lined up in front of an
officer. With a wave of his gloves
he decided who should live
and who should die.
My group was sent to the right.
We were not yet condemned to die.

But most from our transport
were directed to the left.
We had been locked up for six
days without water and food, and
we did not even have air.

Soldiers with rifles ready to
shoot ordered us to line up,
five in a row, and they held
barking dogs on leashes.
Men in striped uniforms helped
the German soldiers to group us.

We walked on a road between barbed
wires. Our group arrived at a big
building. Our escorts screamed,
"Go inside! Fast!" We entered in
a large hall with benches around
the wall and numbered hooks.

On the wall were signs written
in German and in Hungarian:
"Tie your shoes together."
"Remember your hook number,
to find your clothes quickly."

How organized the Germans were.
What a lie it was. We did not know.
None of us got our clothes back.
Our folded clothes were sent to
German citizens, as bonuses.

Screaming soldiers watched us
undress; our heads were shaved. In
the shower the water in one second
was boiling hot and the next second
it was changed to freezing cold.

We were thirsty, we were hungry.
We stuck out our tongues
to swallow a few drops of water.
It did not matter if it was hot
or cold. The Nazi Germans laughed.
It was fun for them.

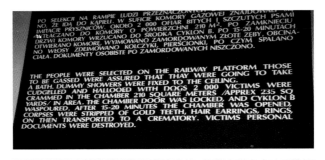

THE PEOPLE WERE SELECTED ON THE RAILWAY PLATFORM THOSE TO BE GASSED WERE ASSURED THAT THAY WERE GOING TO TAKE A BATH. DUMMY SHOWERS WERE FIXED TO THE CEILING. 2 000 VICTIMS WERE CUDGELLED AND HALLOOED WITH DOGS CRAMMED IN THE CHAMBER 210 SQUARE METERS /APPREX 235 SQ YARDS/ IN AREA. THE CHAMBER DOOR WAS LOCKED, AND CYKLON B WASPOURED. AFTER 15-20 MINUTES THE CHAMBER WAS OPENED, CORPSES WERE STRIPPED OF GOLD TEETH, HAIR EARRINGS, RINGS, ON THEN TRANSPORTED TO A CREMATORY. VICTIMS PERSONAL DOCUMENTS WERE DESTROYED.

Roll Call In Birkenau

We were surrounded with barbed wire. In the shadow of four smoky chimneys, all of us had roll call twice a day. It began at daybreak and lasted a few hours.

Midday started the afternoon roll call, and ended when the sun went to sleep. It got dark, so for that day roll call ended. Then Kapo's let us go to sleep.

Our beds were large, made from raw wood, three levels on top of one another. Fourteen women slept on each level. When we moved splinters stuck our bodies.

Fourteen of us had one blanket. There was no space between our tortured bodies. We were like sardines in a can. When one turned, all had to turn.

We slept one head next to a pair of legs. We could smell the other person's feet. Our exhausted, weakened bodies could not take the misery for too long.

On our bodies, we had only a dress, and our shoes were wooden clogs. Often it rained, so we got soaking wet; our bodies couldn't resist for too long. It did not matter that we were young. Many collapsed, and some caught cold.

At every roll call there were selections. The Germans took the weakened away.

Germans were helped by Kapo's. They were collaborators. Kapo's knew the fate of those who were selected.

The ones who were selected forever they disappeared from this hell on earth. They remained within the barbed wire, But they never had another roll call.

In Birkenau, Miri Saved My Life

With other Jews from my hometown we were forced into boxcars and locked in for six days. We had no food, no water, not even air. On Friday, June 2, 1944, the convoy halted. We arrived at Auschwitz-2/Birkenau. The rest was like a horror dream.

Selection!
I was separated from my mother and brother. Dressed in a rag, my feet in wooden clogs*, my head shaved. It rained; it was cold. It was too much for my fifteen-year-old body. On Sunday, June 4, 1944 during roll call I got dizzy. It got dark. I fell on the ground.

When I opened my eyes, Miri, our Block Älteste**, poured some water on my face and she said, "Child, go inside, in the block." Miri saved my life. I was not selected on that day. My parents in heaven watched over my fate.

Miri put me to work. With a piece of brick, I scrubbed the tall chimney's brick all day. With a white bleach gel, with my fingers, I covered the cement between the brick.

In this block were over one thousand young females. Those who worked were permitted to walk; the others had to sit on the crowded three-level beds. Whoever was tall had to bend her neck and head. There was no clean drinking water. We were hungry and thirsty. The water was yellow and rusty. It did not matter that the water was not clean, was bitter and metallic. We were thirsty. Since I worked, I was allowed to walk. Everyone said, "Kis kalyhas (little kiln)*** bring water." So I carried water to the beds all day long.

Sometimes, with a group of girls, we were sent to carry large canisters with food. Close to the distribution place, in the garbage, were piles of dirty potato peels.

When the Kapo looked the other way, we filled our empty stomachs with potato peels. The dirty potato peels helped me to survive.

*Clogs shoes made from wood. **Alteste is overseer appointed by the Germans, Leichner Miri was the daughter of a Rabbi from Bratislava. ***Kis kalyhas means little kin, in Hungarian it sounds very nice, but the English translation does not sound so nice.

Jews From Chechoslovakia

In the summer of 1944,
Jews from Theresienstadt
arrived in Birkenau.

They looked like ghosts.

Men, women, and children
were only skin and bones.

Poor Jews, they were starved
for years in Theresienstadt.

These skeletons hardly moved;
their clothes were infested;
their weakened bodies did
not resist for too long men
carried away the dead daily,
loaded in two rows on a cart,
their stiffened naked bodies
on top of one another.

Men, women, and children.
The dead looked like wood logs.

Those who lived a few more
days ate the green bitter soup,
so called food which was given
to us at Auschwitz-2/Birkenau
in Lager C.

Under the electrified barbed wires
we pushed the bitter, dirty,
green soup through to the
starved Jews from Theresienstadt.

We, the so-called "Hungarian Jews"
could not eat the green soup.

It was bitter and full of sand.

Then one day, Lager C was closed.
We had to stay in our
barracks and the Jews
from Theresienstadt disappeared.

In the Czech Lager were no more
starving, dying Jews.

I asked an adult where they gone?
she said, "they were taken
to warmer climate." I believed her.

The Rooster Is Calling Good Morning!

In my childhood memory there is a popular song which promises hope for Jews: The rooster calls daily, "Good morning, Messiah soon will arrive. The Messiah's legs are green, his wings are shiny gold."

The song ends with the question, "But when the Messiah will come?" In the rooster's song is a promise: Messiah will come to save every Jew. But for unknown reason He did not arrive. The globe closed its heart and eyes.

Very few cared about the fate of forgotten Jews. The sadistic hordes of many European nations, with zeal, helped Nazis to murder Jews. Upon our misery, the collaborators had fun torturing us.

Laughing, they said to Jews, "Messiah didn't come to save you, dirty Jew!" Our parents awaited the Messiah. But He did not arrive to save millions of our brethren as they were gassed in the crematoria of Birkenau.

Their bodies were burned in the ovens, and their ashes used as fertilizer. In the summer of 1944, the arrival of new deportees took on a new scale. The ovens did not have the capacity to burn the massacred bodies. In adjoining forests a huge, deep, ditch for the gassed bodies was dug.

They were thrown in the ditch and burned. After a half century, the ditch was filled with water, so there is a huge, deep lake.*
But the water in this lake is black.

Religious leaders for years have brought bags of white sand from the Holy Land. They tried to clear the water in the lake. Although, for many years, white sand was thrown in the lake, the water does not clear; it remains black.

Around the lake there are a few trees. But in the water not even a fly lives.

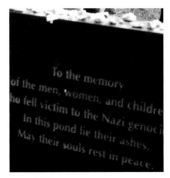

I visited the lake April 23, 1998, spring 1999, spring 2000, and 2004.

Homecoming

After the Second World War,
a few Jews returned with
broken hearts. They were
not welcomed by the locals.

Many families had no survivors.
Still the Hungarian's asked,
"Why were not all Jews killed?"

The city people were void
of sympathy, looted belongings,
and seized properties that were
not returned to their owners.

The surviving orphans were
threatened by Hungarian's.

In the sky, the sun shone bright;
at night the sky had stars
and the moon gave light.

But for the few Jews
who survived in extreme anguish,
it remained forever dark,
a frightful nightmare.

Jewish orphans returned
from the hell with bitter hearts.

They left the city to begin
a new life, but they never
forget the pain of the dark
misery they lived through.

My homecoming was the same as
that of many other orphans.*

I left the lonely, empty house,
the unfriendly locals
and my hometown.

Then I struggled to stand on my
shaky, trembling feet.

My parents house

*Afraid of my own shadow, as a child
with hope, I hid in the shed where
my parents had kept wood for heating.
The tenant yelled at me.
With nothing at home for me, I left my
parents' house and never went back.
Several years later, the house was given
to a Hungarian couple.

Our Daughter

When she was born,
I put a red bow in
her long auburn hair.
She had a round face,
and beautiful blue eyes.

When she did not cry
I would think that
she was a doll,
from a store or a
display in a museum.

When she was nine
months old, she walked
and she balanced
her fragile body
with her small hands.

She was pretty, smart,
and always asked questions.
Why are leaves green?
Why does water have no color?
Why is the milk white?

Her questions never stopped.
At the age of four,
she read tales from books.
When she was five,
she attended
the first year of school.

She remembered every book
she read, without
looking into the book.
She was born witty
and very pretty.

While I walked with her
people stopped to look
at her beautiful face.
I was proud to have
such a pretty child.

She grew to be
a successful woman,
a wife, the mother
of two,
and remains
a loving,
pretty
daughter to us.

Agneta,
the author's
daughter as a teenager

The author's daughter, Agneta, 8 years old
and son Tiberiu, 2, years old

Chibi the Little Chicken!

Mother Hen has nineteen chicks.
They are covered with yellow puffs.
Some chicks have dark spots.
The chicks are always hungry
and they are always cold.

The little chicks are hiding,
under Mother's wings and tummy.
She keeps them warm. Nineteen
chicks are too many and is
crowded under Mother Hen.

To get under Mother's protection,
the stronger chick pushes out
the weak ones. Mother Hen cannot
protect them all at once, so she
must move right and left to warm
them all.

With her constant moving,
an accident occurs.
She steps on a chick's leg.
Mother Hen accidently breaks
a little chick's fragile leg.

Our son is five years old and
he runs to help the injured chick.
He prepares matches with a string.
The boy puts a cast on the chick's
leg. To keep it warm,
he puts it under his shirt.

He places the chick in a large
basket, and he often feds the
little chick. He names the puffy
chick "Chibi." And, when he
leaves for kindergarten made sure
the chick is warm and fed.

"Chibi" grows fast, her leg heals, and she does not fit in the basket. She is put out with the other chicks, but Chibi is not happy among them and waits at the door for the boy to come home.

The boy brings "Chibi" into the house, and puts her in front of the mirror. Chibi, the chick starts to sing. "Chip, chip. chip," and our son is happy that he cured the chick.

Tiberiu, the author's son between chickens.

Left Our Homeland for the Unknown

With tremendous effort we moved to a big city. Our new home had a large garden. I dug holes in the back yard to plant forty assorted fruit trees and thirty roses in the front yard.

When they bloomed, it warmed my heart. I felt flowers and trees grow and bloom from my blood.

Unexpectedly, one day we got visas to leave our native country, our city, our home, our garden. The man who got our house demanded some changes in the house.

To get visas, and to giveaway our home, by law, we had to pay the city for the changes, for painting the house.

The city took possession of our property without any compensation. With worry about the unknown, we gave away the key to our house.

Left our homeland for the unknown, with no valuables, no money. The two children were all our wealth.

Many sleepless nights in Italy, we waited six months to get visas to enter the United States of America. We arrived on March 17, 1966.
It was St. Patrick's Day.

Everyone celebrated this holiday,
but we did not. Our worry contin-
ued. Where do we sleep, how do we
feed the kids? No language,
no home, where do we go?

In a new country, what we will do?
With time, our worry passed.
It did not matter that we
worked sixteen hours a day.
Our struggle gave the children
a better life.

Bless the day we got to the
United States of America!
America is the best country
in the world.

Going to College

In my youth,
I had no chance
for a higher education.
When opportunity came in
the United States of America,
I registered at a college.

My English wasn't the best
and my pronunciation
was a disaster.
In my first year,
I had to repeat
the English class.

For us who were born in foreign
lands, it takes
tremendous effort to speak
and write English.

In the English language,
you swallow some words.
You do not read every letter,
or you pronounce them
in a different way.

But I must learn;
I am in a College.

Often I asked my professors
for advice and help.
How I quit school?

Their encouragement kept me going.

We live in the United States,
in this beautiful country.

If we don't understand English
we are not real Americans.

There were not too many
grannies in my classes.
It was hard to attend school
with a much younger generation.

But I made it.

The Golden Age

Why do people always say,
"It's good to reach
the golden age?"
Our body is tired; it's worn.
So our old age is not golden.

When we are old, it hurts
everywhere. Sickness takes its
toll on the elderly
and some are stricken very hard
when they reach their "golden age."

In their youth, most elders
worked seven days a week
and saved money for a house
for their golden age.

The government takes care
of those who used up
all their earnings, when
they get to their golden age.

Some had an easy life,
never worked too much never saved,
they get free medication
and food stamps when they
arrived at their golden age.

We, who worked hard, must pay for
our medication, food
and every need we have, from
our savings for the golden age.

Like vulture above their prey,
city and state governments
tax on our saved earnings,
saved for our golden age.

The young do not appreciate
the sacrifice their parents made,
or the hard work, to save for their
children's better golden age.

When Stricken By A Stroke

None of us expect to get
a stroke.* It strikes uninvited,
when it arrives, and it knocks
you hard, without mercy,
off your feet.

You become a baby in your bed,
cannot see, nor sit in your bed,
nor walk, nor feed yourself.
A cloud is over your family's
head.

Tragedy hits, covers your life,
no medicine or doctor can help.
Your body is stricken
with a stroke, and your
family suffers the most.

continued

Your family helplessly tries
to comfort your stricken body.
For them it is difficult to cope
and see you in this phase.

If you are one who survives
a stroke, you must learn
to walk again, to talk,
to eat by yourself.

Gradually you began to see,
and learn again to read.
You need constant help every day.
The recovery is very slow.

You are as a newborn child
who begins to walk
and talk. On trembling feet,
you try to walk,
and nothing is easy.

And you have constant
pain in your knee.
Physical therapy
and medication doesn't help.

And nothing is easy - -
to get up from a chair,
to take a shower.
Someone must prepare your food
and medication.

You try to help wash the dishes,
but forget how to use a sponge.
You wash dishes with a spoon
or knife; with a rag you
try to sweep the floor.

The way you were,
it is a miracle
then you can walk,
put on your clothes,
shave, eat, and see to read.

In time, you,
and us hope that
your speech returns.
The daily therapy might will
help you to express yourself.

*On January 7, 1999 Ernest, my husband ,
had a stroke. He can't talk or write and
hardly walks. With therapy we try to
improve his health and with time we hope
things may improve.

In Memory of Our Martyrs

For years, in the news untold
stories began to be written.
Aged witnesses' began to testify
about the Holocaust.

Readers acquire knowledge
of those who were massacred
and those who survived.
some survivors were silent
for over fifty years.

Yet, some had the courage to talk,
and tell the horror they lived
through, so the next generation
would remember our Martyrs.

I'm sorry that I agreed to talk,
but my mother would say,
"You my child, must tell others,
not to forget what happened to us."
My Mother would say,
"If you are silent,
others will never know."

My Mother would continue,
"How hard we worked
and how peaceful we were.
G'd will give strength
to tell others how we lived,
and how we were murdered."

"You, my child, must remember
the dark years of our history.
Your generation
is the last who survived.
Remind others to tell their
story, to their children,
to the next generation."

In the memory of our families,
who were brutally murdered,
we who are still alive
have on obligation.
It is our duty to share
our memories with others.

If we remain silent, it is
as if we murder them again.
Let people read
and hear from the witnesses.

Few of us still alive and sometimes we
could hear, "Holocaust could not exist.
For Centuries people on our
Mother Earth are civilized."

My Vision In Sandomierez

On the large stone-paved plaza,
surrounded by nice buildings,
I was listening to a Polish man's
tales.* But it was not a story;
it was true.

It happened in August 1943.
City officials summoned all the
Jewish leaders of the town
for a chat. They forced the
Jews into a truck and took them
into nearby forest. Each ended
up with a bullet in his head.

Jewish leaders had no chance
to warn their families
and other Jews in the town,
to tell them to organize,
to try to fight or run away.

Next day at sunrise, in the early
morning, every Jew in the town had
to come into the paved square:
elderly, women, men, young adults.
Mothers carried their
crying children.

It happened 56 years ago.
How frightened they were.
I feel, hear, their hearts beat.
Not for long could they see
the bright sun in the blue sky.

From the windows, the bastardly
butchers sprayed bullets into
the crowd until everyone
feel to the ground.

For days, blood seeped on the
stone-paved square of Sandomierez.

A few Jews managed to hide
in the tunnel,
but bloodthirsty Poles
went after them.
Locals had no remorse
until all Jews were killed,
but in Sadomierez,
one was spared.

A young boy was sent
by his father to close their door.
As he returned,
the massacre reached its pick.
Poor child, he run to the next
town to tell what he witnessed.

On 4/14/99, I listened the Polish man
story, closed my eyes and visioned the
tragedy which happened many years ago.

Birds In Majdanek

Four birds are on top
of a tall stone pole.
Their wings are knotted together,
with their heads each looking
in different directions.

To the East, to the West,
to the South, to the North -
these birds attempt to fly away
somewhere, anywhere, to escape,
to be as free as other birds.

On the horizon is the city
of Lublin. At night its light
shines. During the daylight
the birds can see
the beautiful city of Lublin.
There other birds fly free.

The city is only minutes away,
but armed guards beat and kill
birds who look that way. The birds
wish for a day or two to visit the
city to heal their wounds.

To get some strength,
to endure the misery they have:
hunger, beatings, daily killing.
The birds wish to get, at least,
a short break from this hell
on earth.

The birds are enclosed in dark
and crowded wooden barracks;
their lives are miserable.
Often they are beaten.

They have no food, no water.
Poor birds, their bloody bodies

are covered with open wounds
and their feathers are torn.
The four birds wish to fly away,
to any four corners on the earth.

Their wings are tangled
with each other's.
They cannot free themselves
to fly East, West, South or North.
All four birds must die
within the enclosing barbed wire.

In memory of prisoners in the Majdanek's concentration camp, there is a statue of four birds, perched on a pole, joined together.

Mother With Her Child

In the blue sky,
the sun shines bright.
But for some it is always dark,
even the bright sunny light.

The sun shines on a stone mother
who would like to save
her child from the certain
death of Zyklon B gas.

Or death by fire
in the heated ovens.
Small children
SS soldiers threw in alive.

A mother with a stone heart
would prefer that G'd
send an angel from heaven
to take her child.

With her arms, the mother
holds up the child
so that the angel can
easily catch her child.

Maybe the angel's wings
are broken and it cannot fly,
to take the child from the
mother's arms into Paradise.

Her child remains free prey
in the sadistic killers' hands.
The mother prays, cries, begs G'd:

"For my sins, do not punish
my child."

"He is innocent,
please have mercy
and send your angel to take him.
Please, G'd, create
a miracle and save this pure,
innocent child."

But the miracle did not happen.
Perhaps the angel could not fly.
In rain or sunshine the statue
of mother and child forever stands.

Majdanek, Poland (1998,1999,2000,2004)

Listen to the Winds!

Tall trees bend in the winds.
Leaves whisper
and birds fly to the open sky.
Those tall trees remember
what they have seen.

The winds whisper that
56 years ago, they witnessed
the local Poles help the Germans,
and force Jews from Tykochin
to get on trucks.

Surrounded by armed
and screaming soldiers,
they arrived in the forest.
Jews were lined up
on the side of three ditches.

Men, women, young adults,
and mothers who covered
children's eyes, so as not
to see the deadly guns.
With no mercy, they were shot
until all fell into a ditch.

The butchers had their feast.
Some Jews were mortally wounded,
but the killers did not
want to waste another bullet;
they let Jews suffer until death.

Listen to the winds. Trees bend
and remember what they had seen
when all Jews from the small town
of Tykochin were murdered.
They lay in three common graves.*

Trees get new leaves each year,
grass covers the ground
and birds fly over the graves.
But the Jews of Tykochin are gone.
Even now Tykochin looks as
a ghost town.

A child, an eleven-year-old boy,
fell into a small hole,
and by a twist of fate or miracle
he survived, having witnessed how
Jews from Tykochin were killed.

I visited the graves, 1998,1999,2000,2004

Treblinka

Janus Korczak ran the orphanage in
the Warsaw Ghetto and chose to go with
children to Treblinka rather than accept
the Underground's offer to rescue him.

The name "Treblinka" is impressive.
One would think of a Polish city or
town where people live in harmony,
children play and go to school.

Each spring green grass, tall trees
and colorful flowers show the beauty
of Polish land. In the winter a white
blanket covers the meadow.

Amidst nature's beauty, there is a narrow
partially paved two-way road which
gradually changes to one-way and ends
on an unimaginable field. On the side
of the road, at about a distance of every
two meters, are concrete bars.

They look like picnic tables on the ground
or people to relax on weekends.
Big "umbrella" trees spread shade over
the large cement blocks. Grass and
colorful flowers cover the ground.

In this picturesque place during the
Second World War, a concentration camp
was hidden where Nazis, Polish and
Ukrainian collaborators brought Jews of
Poland's cities and small settlements to
murdered. Jews in Poland were
killed like flies.

In Treblinka Janus Korczak holding
orphans' hands went with them to death.
In Treblinka's grassy field and trees,

as an aftereffect of heavy rain or melting snow, fragments of human bone grow like mushrooms. One never knew when a bone fragment will appear.

In memory of those who perished, seventeen thousand stones are placed on a huge field. Their size varies as large or as small as the town's Jewish population was. Some cities' names are painted on stones.

1.

2.

3.

1.In the center of Treblinka is a memorial and in front is a chilling field of human bones/ashes covered with tar. 2. J. Korczak 3.Stones commemorate the wiped out towns.

(Not) Every Life Returns to Birkenau

A snail slowly crawls
on the grassy ground in Birkenau.
The snail is not afraid to crawl.
She can have a feast on the grass.
but over a half of century ago
a snail did not crawl in Birkenau.

The snail would have been a feast
to the hungry starving inmates.
On the grassy ground there
are frogs and bugs jumping.
Half a century ago nature was dead.
There was no grass on the ground.

Every spring, nature renews itself;
life begins. Butterflies and birds
fly in the clear sky. Snails crawl,
frogs and bugs jump. The snail
crawls on the top of the blown up
crematorium.

Butterflies and birds fly over
the camp's remnants.
Yearly, young Jewish children
come to visit Auschwitz-2/Birkenau.
They witness the cemetery where
there are no gravestones.

From around the globe Jews
come to say Kaddish* in Birkenau.
In Birkenau millions of Jews were
tortured, gassed and burned, their
ashes used to fertilize
these huge killing fields.

Snails, frogs, bugs, birds
and butterflies renew life
each year in Birkenau. They can
have a feast on the grassy ground.
The inmates' lives were cut short
and they can never return.

We Jews come from many parts
of the world to ease our pain.
We light candles in memory
of our families, our martyrs,
and with sorrow we leave Birkenau.

*Kaddish: Jewish hymn in praise of G'd;
mourner's prayer for the dead
crematorium's 2, 3, 4, 5 were
in Auschwitz-2/Birkenau

My Heart Aches

The Hungarian's were eager to
solve what they called, "The
Jewish problem." They wanted to
get a free hand looting every
Jewish home. From Hungary we Jews
were shipped with great speed,
about a half million in a month.

In Auschwitz-2/Birkenau the
four crematoria could not
burn our loved ones.
The murderers threw our gassed
brethren to burn in a deep ditch.
I feel my dear mother and brother
were thrown into that ditch.
My heart hurts and always aches.

When I accidentally cut or
hit myself, a sharp pain follows,
a sharp pain which in time
eventually heals and doesn't
leave a lasting mark.
But my heartache is a constant
shadow in my life day and night.

To ease my pain I participated
in the "March of the Living"*
with teenagers a few times.
I wish to forget the history
of my past and the nightmares
I constantly have.

They follow me when I am awake
during the day and will follow
me to my grave.

In my dream I see the Ash Pond's black water in Birkenau and my heart beats fast. It is pumping so strong that it hurts, as if it is ready to jump out of my chest.

In my dream I see my mother floating on that water, holding my brother in her arms. She smiles beautifully and they are both waving at me. I hear them say, "Do not follow us."

*March of Living: a program to teach Jewish history to Jewish youth a two-week trip to Poland and Israel. Survivors and teenagers participate.

The Grss is Green

Now in Auschwitz-2/Birkenau
the grass is green.
Each little blade of grass
grows on our families' blood
and we step on the green grass.

While we walk on the grass
we do not think that the grass
grows on the ashes of our
relatives. If the grass
could talk it would say to us,
"Do not step on me,
because I am green grass
and I grow from someone's ashes."

In the years if 1940 to 1945
grass did not grow in
Auschwitz-2/Birkenau.
There was only sand and stone
and always freezing rain.
The rain chilled our bones.
We did not have warm clothes.

Even inside in the wooden
barracks, it was always cold.
In the 1940's German soldiers,
with barking dogs and rifles
ready to shot, made sure
no one escaped the crematoria's
gas chambers.

To us who lived through the
terror of the concentration
camps, to our aching heart,
the change we witness brings
great feeling.

We did not think that one day
the time would come that we
could walk freely from Auschwitz 1
to Auschwitz-2/Birkenau on the
guarded road.

Now, Polish police watch with care
that none of us should get hurt,
The change of history is great,
even though we step on
blood-stained grass.

gazowymi. Ponad 450 bohaterskich więźniów zostało zamordowanych przez esesmanów w trakcie buntu oraz w odwet za jego zorganizowanie.

On October 7, 1944, members of the Sonderkommando - the special detachment of Jewish prisoners who were forced to empty the gas chambers after a mass gassing and undertake the burning of the corpses - organized the only armed revolt that ever took place at Auschwitz.
They succeeded in destroying Gas Chambers and Crematorium IV. More than 450 heroic prisoners who took part in the revolt were murdered by the SS, either during the revolt itself or subsequently for the purpose of retaliation.

ב-7 באוקטובר 1944 פתחו אנשי ה״זונדרקומאנדו״ היהודים במרד מאורגן. אסירים אלה השתייכו לפלוגה מיוחדת, שחבריה

The Long Row of Blue Jackets!

At the sound of the shofar* I became
very emotional that we Jews
can freely walk on the paved road.
From the Auschwitz main camp I walk
to Auschwitz-2/Birkenau, on
the three kilometer road,
I walk with my fellow marchers.

We are a large group of teenagers
and a few survivors.
We survivors age quickly.
We won't walk for too long.
The trip to Poland is tiring,
very emotional and heart-wrenching.

It gives me strength to see
the large group of teenagers.
They came from many countries,
I am proud to walk with them.
It eases my pain that I can share
my bitter experiences.

I tell these lovely
Jewish teenagers my past history.
Now they can tell their
grandchildren, the Jews history.
They can say they heard from me
and other survivors.

We walk from Auschwitz-1
to Auschwitz-2/Birkenau quietly.
The young try to help the old.
All of us wear blue jackets.
It is heart-warming to see
long rows of blue jackets.

Proudly I wear my blue jacket.
When we reached the small hill,
there is a bridge with a small
curb. I look around.
There were only blue jackets.

What revenge we give to the past
killers. We are a nation.
We are here. We are stronger.

We Jews survived against all odds.

*Shofar ran's horn blown during the High Holidays. The liturgy instructing Jews to hear the shofar is followed by a blessing that G'd has permitted us reach the day.

The Little Lonely Child

In the center of this photo,
a little child sits alone.
On the road he sits by himself.
Perhaps his siblings were directed
to the right, so he remained alone.
Poor little lonely, hungry boy.
He sits like a little puppy.

He is waiting for his relatives.
Maybe his mother or grandmother,
or the person in whose care he was
left. In this mad world he is a lost
little boy who is scared
and forgotten by everyone.

In the photo are other children
and adults who are condemned to die
in the gas chambers of Birkenau.
By the Nazi standards they have no
value. They are young mothers
with young children.

Why in the world did no one
care that this happened?
Why were all these beautiful young
mothers and children murdered?
Their only crime is that they were
born Jewish, so by the SS
and collaborators they must die.

On the entire globe has everyone
gone mad? Every nation closes its
eyes and ears. No one wants to
hear the Jewish people cry. When
SS soldiers with barking dogs and
rifles ready to shoot, order the

group to move, I can imagine
the little frightened boy.
He does not understand the command.

Perhaps a Nazi soldier kicks
him with his boots. The poor
little boy does not understand why
everything was changed around him;
Why was he left alone?
No one kisses him; no one hugs
him; no one feeds him. In the
center he is waiting for his
siblings.

Maybe the Nazi soldier throws him
on a cart pulled by men, on top or
between the old, sick and dead.
Maybe he was pushed into the gas
chamber, or into everburning ditch.

Hopefully he did not suffer long.

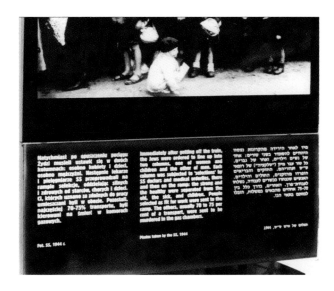

Letter to My Mother

Although many years have passed since we have seen each other my dear mother, I always see your beautiful face and smile. I feel your love for your two children.

Father was drafted into forced labor, and you Mother, were struggling very hard to make ends meet. Around the world, a mother like you would have deserved a Nobel Prize.

The last time we spoke was on Friday. It was June 2, 1944. Upon our arrival to Auschwitz-2/Birkenau, during that turmoil you, Mommy, asked me, "Should I give your brother to the care of our neighbor?"

You continued, "She has three children between the ages one and four." I answered, "I am fifteen and brother is five years old I can take care of myself better than a little boy."
It took less than a minute.

With a wave of the hand, I was pushed to the right, and we did not see each other again. Because of my love for my little brother and you, my dear mother, you were gassed, and you were only thirty seven years old. My poor little brother died in your arms.

He was not a lonely frightened
child. The two of you entered
into heaven. I hope you meet Daddy
in the heaven and the three
of you are waiting for me.

You, Mommy, died not knowing that
the Hungarian's murdered Daddy
in the spring of 1943 on the Russian
front. The Hungarian government
did not notify our family
of Father's death.

Daddy doesn't have a grave site,
nor you Mommy, nor my brother.
To honor tragic past with
large group of teenagers I have
visited Auschwitz-2/Birkenau
a few times.

The famous Black Lake and the
crematorium ruins are the only
grave site.

Whose Hair Is On Display

Behind a glass wall a huge pile
of grey hair is on display.
It's the silent witness of the
treachery done by Nazis.

There must be a train-load,
or perhaps two truck
of grey hair on display.
Whose hair is collected
behind that large glass wall?

Our Martyrs' hair turned grey,
because their heads were shaved,
after they were murdered with
Zyclon B gas in the gas chambers.
My mother's hair was wavy, black.

She was gassed on the day we
arrived in Auschwitz-2/Birkenau.
It was June 2, 1944. Is my
mother's hair in that pile?

The large piles of hair are the
silent witnesses of Nazi crimes.
The Martyrs were robbed of their
possessions, even after death.

In Poland, Auschwitz-1, Block
18, on the second floor, behind
a large glass wall there are piles
of grey hair on the display.

Old and young hair was used by
the Nazi war machinery.
Human hair in large sacks were
transported into Germany.

Hair was used for mattresses
and was woven into materials.
Then it was given as blankets
to the faithful Nazi believers.

My hair was long and blond.
It was braided in two ponytail.
My head was shaved, so my blond
hair did not change its color.

Maybe it was woven with other
slaves' hair for blankets.
Did those who received the
blankets know that it was made
from slaves' hair?

Hair of the victims, found after the
liberation on the camp site.

Luggage Is the Silent Witness!

Austria, Belgium and Holland were under Nazi SS occupation. Every country under Nazi oppression was ruled by the Gestapo's office.

The Gestapo ordered Jews to pack their valuables into a small piece of luggage, because they were to be resettled. The people were told to, "Bring the tool you need to work in your trade."

Further Jews were told, "Make a list of your possessions, so no one can take your valuables." Germans were a trustworthy nation.

Nazis were masters of misleading people. In each occupied country there were local collaborators who helped the Nazis. Jews hurried to banks to withdraw their money, jewelry, documents, paintings other valuables and necessary tools.

Carefully they were packed in carry-on luggage. Doctors put in medications; tailors, needles; shoemakers, hammers; lawyers, typewriters. Locksmiths and carpenters packed tools.

On arrival in Auschwitz-2/Birkenau, as Jews disembarked from the boxcars they were directed to the gas chambers, murdered and cremated. Jews never saw their carefully packed luggage. The Nazis used the packed valuables for their war expenses.

Jews' tools and instruments were carefully sorted, packed and then shipped into Germany.

When the war was coming to an end the Nazi SS soldiers had no time to destroy the leftover luggage. So luggage remains the silent witness, to the treachery of the Nazi's crimes.

The shameful past can be seen on display. In Poland, Auschwitz-1, in Block 18, on the second floor there are many victims' luggage. Some wrote an inventory of the content of their luggage.

Symphony Music in Birkenau.

On arrival to Birkenau from all countries, Jews heard soft music. An orchestra played a symphony.

The players wore striped rags. They were pale, but they played beautifully on their instruments. The players were well known musicians in their respective countries.

When the musicians arrived in Birkenau they were selected for a special task. Their music was supposed to mislead and calm the newcomers to this killing fields.

As the long row of box cars rolled in, day and night with new deportees, the musicians played symphony music. SS soldiers and Kapos screamed, dogs barked, families separated, children cried, and men whispered.

It was strange to hear the music. Those musicians greeted many victims to whom the symphony music was the last calming memory. It gave them some relief before they were murdered.

In the spring of 1944, in one month about half a million deportees arrived. Large transports came, especially from Hungary and the other countries which were invaded by Hungarian's.

Jews came from the former Czechoslovakia, Serbia, and the Romania's Transylvania. My family and I arrived from occupied Romania.

Since 1944 a question often comes to my mind, about those who played music as new deportees arrived. Did any member of the orchestra survive the Holocaust? Did they testify about their misery, experience, and the selections?

The musicians lived through hell by knowing what the fate was of every person who was directed to the left. Selection to the right meant temporary survival for about one to two percent of the new arrivals.

This is my true testimony; we were over 95 people squeezed in the cattle/box car. In that car, a child was born; a few people died. At the last second only I was directed to the right.

A Former Paratrooper

On November 22, 1999, I waited
on the line to be served.
Suddenly a man began to talk,
and he proudly said, "In Germany,
at the age of eighteen,
I volunteered to serve my country.
I was a paratrooper in the army and
fought through to the end."

To me, as a Holocaust survivor,
his statement was too much.
It was more than I could swallow.
Gasping for air, I finally said,
"You fought against our beautiful
country, the United States. Why did
you come here? Germany is your
country. You served the murderers,
of European nations; Why you are in
America?" The former paratrooper's
eyes were flashing. He got angry,
but kept quiet.

I could hardly compose myself
and thought, "How a man who helped
to burn towns, who served the
murderers of innocent people; how
can he live and prosper among us?
As a paratrooper he served, among
the first group of those soldiers
who invaded other nations' lands.
Maybe the German Government,
is rewarding him with a pension.

This man killed American soldiers.
Why does a former murderer live
here? How did he get visa to enter
into the United States of America.
Who was his accomplice? Who is he,
American or Nazi?"

Celebration in Cesarea

The emotional journey in Poland ended. From around the world Jewish children, chaperons and small groups of survivors of the Shoah* arrived in Israel.

Israel is every Jews homeland no matter part of world we live in. Israel, small but strong, is the pride of every Jew in the four corners of the earth.

There were over seven thousand in our group. We arrived to celebrate the anniversary of the Declaration of Israel Independence. The celebration was held in Cesarea. The festival was organized on the seashore and there was a cool breeze from the sea. There were tables with chairs and a variety of hot & cold food. Plenty soft drinks and ice cream.

The most memorable event was the celebration of young Jewish children dancing on the theater's stone paved floor, which was built by the Romans one thousand years ago. Around the theater's floor were stone benches, where the Romans watched shows years ago. Now, on the floor Jewish children were singing and dancing. The change in history provides a great feeling.

At the closing ceremony
"Hatikvah"** was played.
The music and the voices of over
seven thousand people singing.
Tears were streaming from my eyes.
I wished to hear the song again.

I was so happy to see Jewish
children celebrating in the
former Roman theater of Cesarea.
G'd helped the Jews, to have
a country, a State which protects
us around the world.
I enjoyed the change in history.
I tried to forget the tiring
long trip in Poland:
the emotions on the blood soaked
grass, the Ash Pond with its black
water, and the concentration camps.

* Shoah: Holocaust, **Hatikvah Israel's
national anthem, "The Hope" when
translated into English

My Husband's Story

This is a true story about my husband's youth, and others who were born in Europe, especially in Hungary and part of other countries which were invaded by Huns.

In 1942 the Hungarian government drafted Jews between the ages of 18 to 55. Ernest was 21 years old. Young men were forced to work hard labor. They were beaten. Without food, warm clothes. They slept

outside in the frozen snow. During the cold nights some froze to death. From the original group over 90% died. They were forced on foot to walk to Polish lands and into the Russian tundra. At the end of 1943 the Hungarian/Germans were pushed back from Poland and Russia. The handful of the young men on foot were forced by armed soldiers to retreat to Hungary. Those who were still alive were placed in a shed in the city of Balf, at the Austria's' Hungary border. They had typhus, high fevers for days. My husband lost consciousness. When he awoke, he crawled from the place he had been laying for some time. He remembers, "I rolled a stick on the blanket; the lice on it were as thick as the blanket. In a few days we were forced to walk again. Those who could not walk were shot on the spot." In the history it is known as "The Death March." He continued, "Few survivors got to Austria's Dachau, Mauthausan, Gurnskichen & Welsh." The skeleton like survivors were liberated by Allied Forces on May 6, 1945. Slowly they went home. There was no family, just empty homes. Every household belonging had been ransacked. The handful of survivors worked hard. They tried to put their broken lives together. The young got married and raised families. Each survivor was marked by that hard time.

This is not fiction. This happened in my husband's youth. The author married Ernest in June, 24, 1946.

EPILOGUE.

I am from județul Sălaj and the city of ȘIMLEU-SILVANIEI. I was born on February 14, 1929, when the Depression in Europe was getting worse. Poor and middle class families had to choose whether to buy clothes, a pair of shoes or feed their children.

During the Hungarian invasion, I kept a diary about how our lives changed and how best friends turned away from us only because we were born Jewish. After the war, I returned home with a hope that our lives will became normal. I was 16 years old, but everything disappeared: my parents, my brother and my relatives. Our home was empty. When I received the information that I lost everyone and everything, I could not think or talk for a long time. I asked myself how our G'd allowed so many lives to be extinguished. I wanted to believe that my parents in the heaven prayed and watched over my fate, but many times I had doubts.

After WWII, I wished to leave a written memory of my parents so they should not be forgotten. Since we lived under Communist rule, I thought this memorial would cause suspicion. In my poems, I briefly touched many major events of my life. By writing these poems, my goal was to leave something about our past lives to the present and future generations.

I was married at age of 17 to Ernest who is a survivor of various forced labor camps and the Death March.

We lived under Communist rule in Rumania from 1946-1966. We dreamed of leaving Rumania, but for many years it remained a dream. Finally, we received our visas and left Rumania.

In the United States each New Year passes quickly. With my husband of 54 (when the book was first printed now is 59) years our lives were not easy. In spite of everything, we raised and educated two children. We need only our health. In spite of all our hardship, we have survived.

Forever my thanks and my gratitude to Milberg Weiss Berhard Hynes & Lerach LLP for reminding the world of the past misery Jews suffered in Europe from 1934-1945. My appreciation to Deborah M. Sturman, Esq. for selecting me from the Shoah testimony. I am honored that Prof. Burt Neuborne, Esq. analyzed my interview on 60 minutes on November 29, 1998. I am with great respect the meeting I had with Mr. Melvyn I. Weiss, Esq. and Lois Silverman. Mr. Weiss introduced me to the media when we started the action against Volkswagen. I had told him that I had written poems. He read them to Ms. Silverman and me.
I was moved and grateful.

With Thanks,

Elly Gross